EMPOWERED

TEEN INK

Edited By Sarah Waterhouse

First published in Great Britain in 2022 by:

Young Writers
Remus House
Coltsfoot Drive
Peterborough
PE2 9BF
Telephone: 01733 890066
Website: www.youngwriters.co.uk

All Rights Reserved
Book Design by Ashley Janson
© Copyright Contributors 2021
Softback ISBN 978-1-80015-785-9

Printed and bound in the UK by BookPrintingUK
Website: www.bookprintinguk.com
YB0493S

⭐ FOREWORD ⭐

Since 1991, here at Young Writers we have celebrated the awesome power of creative writing, especially in young adults where it can serve as a vital method of expressing their emotions and views about the world around them. In every poem we see the effort and thought that each student published in this book has put into their work and by creating this anthology we hope to encourage them further with the ultimate goal of sparking a life-long love of writing.

Our latest competition for secondary school students, Empowered, challenged young writers to consider what was important to them. We wanted to give them a voice, the chance to express themselves freely and honestly, something which is so important for these young adults to feel confident and listened to. They could give an opinion, share a memory, consider a dilemma, impart advice or simply write about something they love. There were no restrictions on style or subject so you will find an anthology brimming with a variety of poetic styles and topics. We hope you find it as absorbing as we have.

We encourage young writers to express themselves and address subjects that matter to them, which sometimes means writing about sensitive or contentious topics. If you have been affected by any issues raised in this book, details on where to find help can be found at www.youngwriters.co.uk/info/other/contact-lines

CONTENTS

Al-Islah Girls' High School, Blackburn

Khulaybah Mahroosh (11) & Hafsa	1
Aalia Dhorat (11)	2
Aisha Aden (12) & Khadija Hussein (11)	4
Irfah Ahmed (11)	6
Juwayriyah Hussain (11)	7
Halima Ali (12)	8
Safiyyah Mulla (11)	9
Hijab Khalid (13) & Mehak	10
Laibah Waseem (11) & Sarmina Najeeb (12)	11
Hafsah Mulla (11)	12
Izba Ahmed (13)	13
Laiba Hussain (11) & Aisha Hussain (11)	14
Maryam Nisar (11)	15
Aamna Zafar (13)	16
Arayshah Rashid (11)	17
Dua Nawaz (11)	18

Fernhill School, Farnborough

Tayanna Rai (12)	19
Leona Gurung (12)	20
Cailin Vimpany (12)	22
Kieren Houlton (12)	23
Amber Gurung (13)	24
Arabella Ash-Nicholson (13)	25
Bethany Hawksworth (12)	26
Callum Edwards (13)	27
Morgan Kendall (13)	28
Shristi Gurung (12)	29
Jessica Shrestha (12)	30
Leah Wheaton (12)	31
Mariana Pires (12)	32
Gracie Langford (12)	34
Elizabeth Evans-Holmes (12)	35
Sophie Morris (13)	36
Lily Cannon (13)	37
Harshil Kumar (12)	38
Izzie Roake (12)	39
Oliver Lomax (12)	40
Rhianna Fitch (14)	41
Kayden Forder (11)	42
Dylan Harris (11)	43
Lexy Musa (12)	44
Sambou-Lamin Jallow (12)	45
Adam Collins (13)	46
Millie James (12)	47
Vanessa Kaliszewska (12)	48
Leyland Forder (13)	49
Kye Nielsen (12)	50
Angel Wood (12)	51
Rachel Gurung (12)	52
Caleb Findlay	53
David Gibson (12)	54
Demi Atherton (12)	55
Max Howells (11)	56
Isis Feldschreiber (12)	57
Skye Scoular (12)	58
Brooke-Siobhan Boyd (13)	59
Brooklyn Creed (12)	60
Lucy Smith (13)	61
Tallulah Carter (13)	62
Siyanna Booth	63
Daria Gheorghe (12)	64
Sarah Grainger (12)	65
Hayley Atkins-Ramsey (12)	66

Anthony Williams (13)	67
Edward Hinder-Humphrey (13)	68
Jack Packer (12)	69
Jacob Harrison (11)	70
Reilly-Jay Sim (12)	71
Lilly Archibald (11)	72
Daniel Jordan (12)	73
Harry Badland (11)	74
Kristiyan Traychevski (13)	75
Jesse Galati (12)	76
Oliver Craven (12)	77
Maisy-Mai Johnson (11)	78
Diba Ghafoori (13)	79
Alfie Taylor Coughlan (11)	80
Mia Ashwood (12)	81
Jack White (12)	82
Billy Ribton (13)	83
Skye Standing (12)	84
Holly Miller (12)	85
Syona Thapa (11)	86
Zack Collins (11)	87
Brandon Munyanyiwa (13)	88
Evie Thompson (11)	89
Rocco Cree (13)	90
Erin Slater (11)	91
Ellie McAughey (12)	92
Nada Asabam (12)	93
Nyla Gorvett (11)	94
Kai Hughes (11)	95
Lily Smith (11)	96
Charlotte Rimell (13)	97

Seva School, Coventry

Ashmeet Kaur (13)	98
Laila Heer (12)	100
Eashar Singh (13)	101
Annanya Gupta (12)	102
Ria Virat (13)	104
Savneet Singh (13)	105
Kataar Singh Khalsa (12)	106
Zakariye Bile (11)	108
Raman Kaur Bains (13)	109
Khushmeet Brar (13)	110

Jasjeevan Bhachu (12)	111
Theresa Nakidde (14)	112
Ajooni Kaur Bahra (13)	113
Heavenpreet Kaur (11)	114
Rajinder Gill (12)	115
Sophie Teplicka (11)	116
Reetdeep (11)	117
Avleen Mann (12)	118
Robert Chiscan (11)	119
Ekamjot Kaur (14)	120
Eesha Kaur	121
Arjun Dhillon (12)	122
Jaya Kaur (11)	123
Jugraj Singh Bening (12)	124
Austin Jaison (11)	125
Manreet Baidwan (12)	126
Benjamin Doherty (11)	127
Jeevan Kaur (11)	128
Gurmehar Maan (12)	129
Gursheen Kaur (11)	130
Dev Atwal (13)	131
Bailee Humphrey (13)	132
Zayed Al-Aamery (11)	133

The Khalsa Academy Wolverhampton, Ettinghshall

Maninder Bains (12)	134
Sukhmanpreet Preet Singh (14)	136
Lorena Mihai (11)	138
Aanya Mahey (12)	139
Ritika Kumari (14)	140
Ravneet Kaur (15)	142
Harleen Kaur (14)	144
Vanshvir Singh (11)	145
Sharan Kaur (17)	146
Parminder Kaur (11)	147
Chanpreet Chouhan (11)	148
Simran Kaur (11)	149
Ishaan Singh Aujla (11)	150
Jassraj Singh (11)	151
Armaandeep Patara (13)	152
Paramveer Singh (11)	153
Aditya Singh (11)	154

Treorchy Comprehensive School, Pengelli

Summer Button (14)	155
Layla Van Zijl (13)	156
Jamie-Lee Taylor (15)	158
Molly-Jo Carmichael (13)	160
Kayleigh Perry (14)	162
Ella Davies (15)	164
Cecilia Horvath-Vass (12)	166
Leo Lanciotti (13)	167
Lilien Horvath-Vass (12)	168
Millie Hislop (14)	169
Ieuan Jones (14)	170
Katie Williams (14)	171
Trystan Rogers (13)	172

THE POEMS

What Would I Change About The World?

What would I change about the world?
Where could I start? There are so many things,
Problems don't fly away like birds with wings,
Anything can be possible, anything.

If I had the power,
Bullying would be finished by the hour
And racism wouldn't be a thing,
Anything can be possible, anything.

In this world, there is disorder,
We shall put an end to murder,
We shall put a stop to smoking,
Anything can be possible, anything.

Success is what we aim for,
What I wish is to stump the war,
Why should animals die because of our mess?
This is what I wish to change about the world,
We can stop all of this by being
More careful and kind to each other.

Khulaybah Mahroosh (11) & Hafsa
Al-Islah Girls' High School, Blackburn

Space

Remember, there's a place called outer space,
It will help you with your pace,
Let's have haste,
Don't waste.

Remember, you're not alone,
Don't trust your phone,
From this place we flee,
We don't need to see.

Remember, this is vital,
Think of the title,

Remember, when you need space,
There's always a place!

Remember, you are the best,
This is not a test!
You are asking me why,
I do not lie,

Remember, there's no limit to your joy,
It's not a toy,
Life is not as easy as it may seem,
Sometimes we need a team,
Not everything is independent,
Sometimes you just need to be an attendant,

Remember, there's a place called outer space,
It will help you with your pace,
Let's have haste,
Don't waste.

Aalia Dhorat (11)
Al-Islah Girls' High School, Blackburn

Dear Mom And Dad

Dear Mum and Dad
I'm here to say
I appreciate you in every way.
You've taken care of me
since the first day.

Dear Moum and Dad
I cried and I cried
and you hugged me so
tight.

I remember the night
you sat beside me and
never left my sight.

Dear Mum and Dad
I'm so grateful for you
to be in my life
and I never want
you to die.

Don't forget you're
the best at making
chai.

Dear Mum and Dad
I'm not gonna lie, when
you left for work
tears streamed down
my eyes.

I can't imagine
my life without
you.

Aisha Aden (12) & Khadija Hussein (11)
Al-Islah Girls' High School, Blackburn

Being Invisible

What I would do if I were invisible...
I would start off pranking my friend,
I would never want this to end,
I would get away with lots of stuff,
Nothing would be tough,
It wouldn't matter if I flew away,
No one would notice anyway,
I would win every game of hide-and-seek,
I would enjoy my week,
I would go to the candy store
And steal some sweet,
I would go to the Apple store
And get some Beats,
What I would do if I were invisible...

Irfah Ahmed (11)
Al-Islah Girls' High School, Blackburn

Dear 2045

I don't know what to do,
I don't think this is fine,
I don't think I am going to survive,
Dear 2045, I am here to say I am sorry.

Giraffes are endangered,
Rhinos are endangered,
This is all because of us,
There's only one thing we can do and that is pray,
Dear 2045, I am here to say I am sorry.

Canada is burning,
Turkey is burning,
And it's all because of us,
Dear 2045, I am here to say I am sorry.

Juwayriyah Hussain (11)
Al-Islah Girls' High School, Blackburn

This Is For You

I know I am new but I grew for you,
I go through a lot and you care a lot,
To someone I love forever and ever,
This is for you.

Whenever I am sad, you're never mad,
Whenever I make a mess, you make it less,
To someone I love forever and ever,
This is for you.

Whenever it's my birthday, you skip workday,
Whenever I stress you out, you still love me deep inside,
To someone I love forever and ever,
This is for you.

Halima Ali (12)
Al-Islah Girls' High School, Blackburn

Thank You For Everything

Everything I do
Is for you,
There is no one better than you,
You help me when I have the flu.

If I have a nightmare,
You're always there,
I don't need to plead,
You're always there for me.

If I have a tear,
You know I fear.
You are the best
From the rest.

When I mope,
You give me hope,
If I wasn't prepared,
You never glared.

Everything I do
Is for you.

Safiyyah Mulla (11)
Al-Islah Girls' High School, Blackburn

Life

Life has become boring,
It's just like another story,
People have sunk too deep,
They feel very lonely,
People only care about themselves.
Sleep is a distraction,
It's the only way you can get rid of your feelings.
But don't worry, you are not alone.
People are here to support you.
We all go through ups and downs in our lives.
Stay strong and focus on yourself.
Put yourself first and forget about the world.

Hijab Khalid (13) & Mehak
Al-Islah Girls' High School, Blackburn

99 Eyes

99 eyes staring and doing nothing,
99 eyes crying for help,
Governments watching yet doing nothing,
Hate and murder still spreading wide,
It's giving us all such a big fright!

99 eyes, 99 lies,
Justice and freedom never happened twice,
Now we raise a voice and say our choice,

99 eyes and 99 tears,
People's faces full of tears and fears,
Let's not leave the problems up to next... year.

Laibah Waseem (11) & Sarmina Najeeb (12)
Al-Islah Girls' High School, Blackburn

You Are The Best!

When I'm ill, you let me rest,
You help me when I have a test,
You clean up when I make a mess,
You're the best!

On an occasion, you get me dressed,
You're the one who sends me a text,
You cheer me up when I am depressed,
You're the best!

You always make me a morning brew,
You always help me tie my shoe,
All of this is very true,
You're the best!

Hafsah Mulla (11)
Al-Islah Girls' High School, Blackburn

Haunted House

I woke up one day with a mysterious dream
I heard a loud scream
I looked to my right
saw a shadow, saw a light
went to discover what was there
saw something in the air
shivered, panicked and stared
suddenly, the house went quiet
the moonlight began to shine
from the eye of mine
I saw the shadow again
tried to escape
but couldn't find the way
I knew I was trapped.

Izba Ahmed (13)
Al-Islah Girls' High School, Blackburn

You Are My Role Model

To all my teachers,
thank you for being there for me,
you have made me who I want to be,
I look up to you,
you are my role model.

During lockdown,
when there was home learning,
you always helped me,
I look up to you,
you are my role model.

Thank you for everything,
thank you for being there for me,
I really appreciate it,
thank you so much.

Laiba Hussain (11) & Aisha Hussain (11)
Al-Islah Girls' High School, Blackburn

Fear Abandoned

Walking past the tall palm trees,
I saw nothing but a desert.
It had been two terrifying days,
If two more, I would have been desperate.
Looking for my friends,
I shivered as though I may never see them again.
As sunrise hit,
I felt the sweet heat warm me,
as I walked and walked.
I saw them at a distance,
my pace quickened.
Fear of abandonment abandoned.

Maryam Nisar (11)
Al-Islah Girls' High School, Blackburn

Wars

The streets are filled with wars
People have nowhere to go
Gunshots are being heard.
Guns being raised to people's heads
Kids going to bed, never knowing if they're going to wake up again
Mothers crying because they've lost another child
When will this stop?
Let's just make peace.
We are better together
Like one big family.

Aamna Zafar (13)
Al-Islah Girls' High School, Blackburn

That's Why I Love Her

My mum is the best,
She cleans up when I make a mess,
When I am hot, she gives me milkshake,
When it is my birthday, she gets me a cake,
That's why I love her

When I am sad, she makes me happy,
When I was a baby, she changed my nappy,
When I am bad,
She's never mad,
That's why I love her.

Arayshah Rashid (11)
Al-Islah Girls' High School, Blackburn

If I Were A Bird

If I were a bird
I would fly high
I would keep a close eye

If I were a bird
I would have all the power
I would fly in the night
If only I were a bird.

Dua Nawaz (11)
Al-Islah Girls' High School, Blackburn

Imagination

It takes you away,
It takes you somewhere you can rule,
It gives you dreams you can achieve,
Dreams that sound too unreal to be real.

It is what you make it to be,
It is your escape from reality,
It may be somewhere you can call home,
Gives you the place where you can be you.

It contains your real self,
The one you kept hidden from everyone else.
One where no one can judge you,
One where you can do anything without a care.

It gives you your second identity,
It can take you somewhere beautiful,
It gives you something unusual, something unreal,
Contains your escape from the real world.

Even though it contains something magical,
Even though it seems like Heaven,
Even though it gives you what you want,
Don't get adddicted.

Tayanna Rai (12)
Fernhill School, Farnborough

It's Not Fair

Being a girl is tiring.

He chose higher-paying jobs like doctors, lawyers and engineers,
She chose lower-paying jobs like female doctors, female lawyers and female engineers.

It's not fair.

She covered herself up, often hidden away,
"Your skirt is too short,"
"Cover up, your uncle is here."
He stood there, joking with his uncle, being treated like a national treasure.

It's not fair.

She ate messily, taking in huge spoonfuls,
"Pig,"
"A lady should not act like this,"
"Lose weight."

He did the same, taking in mouthfuls,
"Funny,"
"You look silly,"
"Here's more."

It's not fair.

He walked freely in the dark, meeting old friends
She walked, shuddering with a taser in her hand, the same friends catcalling her.

It's not fair.

She had the world against her,
She was 'arrogant', 'loud', 'talkative'
He had the world supporting him
He was 'smart', 'outgoing', 'social'.

It's not fair.

Leona Gurung (12)
Fernhill School, Farnborough

What Do I Wish For?

What do I wish for?
I wish for animals
To have a nice home
With no destruction, and have free roam
Of the places they own,
I wish for captivity and climate change to be all gone.

What do I wish for?
The illnesses, the sadness, too much to behold,
They should be gone, be done,
Like how I was told,
How it would be if cancer cells didn't grow,
I wish that diseases were all gone.

What do I wish for?
My family, they aren't doing too good,
They have no money, a house that is old,
They are sad and ill, with nothing to do,
Nothing that's new,
I wish for money for them because they deserve it.

What do I wish for?
This is what I wish for,
Everything I wish for,
All that I wish for.

Cailin Vimpany (12)
Fernhill School, Farnborough

Dear Grandad

You gave me light when I couldn't see,
you gave me air when I couldn't breathe,
you helped me get through all the bad things,
you made an opening,
we laughed until we could no more,
you always did more and more,
the best you could do to help me through
my childhood.

You were the best,
the best I could have asked for
and I hope you're reading this
and I hope you're smiling
because I can remember your smile
and all the good times,
and how much we all loved you.

Grandad looking down,
knowing we loved him,
I wish you were here with me,
to live all of this with me,
love you, Grandad, with all my heart,
wish you were still here
just like the old us.

Kieren Houlton (12)
Fernhill School, Farnborough

Deep Down

I'm supposed to be absolute perfection,
Able to see an angel as my reflection.
Good grades, pretty face and feminine features,
And be the perfect student for all teachers.

Although she herself was the true angel,
Would take a hit however painful,
A man could also do the same,
But she's the one who lit my flame.

I still wonder what my life would've been
If she was the one I'd ever seen.
Would I want to live miserably with a man
Or live my life to the fullest I can?

But perfection is what I'm required to be,
And that means no woman can stand next to me.
The ones who raised me are the ones I have to satisfy,
Even if I have to give my true self a goodbye.

Amber Gurung (13)
Fernhill School, Farnborough

Magic Wand

If I had a magic wand,
I'd sprinkle little bits of dust around
That give people hope and help,
To stop people feeling worthless and sad.

If I had a magic wand,
I'd sprinkle little bits of dust around
To stop riots, death and discrimination
Because no life should just be overthrown like that.

If I had a magic wand,
I'd sprinkle little bits of dust around
That made someone feel just a little less scared,
Loud bangs and shouts shouldn't make someone feel like having a breakdown.

If I had a magic wand,
I'd sprinkle little bits of dust around,
I'd stop the fear and worry,
The fear and worry that just keeps going around.

Arabella Ash-Nicholson (13)
Fernhill School, Farnborough

Not Good Enough

All my life I've never been good enough
I try and try but nothing goes right
So help me God, do something right
Or I won't be able to come alive

All my life I've never been good enough
All I want to do is go to sleep
Although I can't because I go too deep
Now I'm scared to go to sleep

All my life I've never been good enough
From time to time I lie in bed
Thinking about my life choice
I hope people hear my voice

All my life I've never been good enough
I try to distract myself, I can't because I'm distracted
But don't worry, I don't hate my life
I will keep trying in my time.

Bethany Hawksworth (12)
Fernhill School, Farnborough

Hopes

They can come in all shapes and sizes,
Ones to change the course of history, ones to be great.
All hopes can come at a young age, but there's a catch.
They will remember this poem.

They can be different in all ways,
A champion in sports, a bold discovery they found in space.
Even some of the greats made it this far and you can too.
You just need to remember this poem.

However, some people choose to be cruel to others,
Bad choices and consequences will follow.
There is a fix, however, one to right a wrong.
Just remember this poem.

Wherever I am, in the future, making people happy,
Remember me and remember this poem.

Callum Edwards (13)
Fernhill School, Farnborough

Soulmate

You gave me viability, you gave me affection
You made me pleased, with perfection
And for that, you became my soulmate.

You gave me control, you gave me lustre
You made me positive, like the sun beaming
And for that, you changed me.

You clutched me tight, you told me everything is alright.
You accepted me and I accepted you
And for that, I will always love you.

You are my pride, you are my ride or die.
You told me I'm eminent and stuck to your word
And for that, I cannot be without you.

You are my soulmate
You gave me passion
You made me me
After everything
My heart has melted at the seams.

Morgan Kendall (13)
Fernhill School, Farnborough

Speaking Up

Shaking so fiercely with them all staring at me
Light in my eyes, cameras flashing is all I see
Been waiting for this opportunity to finally happen
To inspire the people who are giving up and who slacken

I am scared that these people don't have the strength to speak up
But this will be life-changing, stop what you're doing, put down your cup
Make sure everyone hears you loud and clear
For those who are drinking, don't give up, life isn't over, and put down your beer

Have a better life than one filled with prison
Tell people even if everyone won't listen
Be who you are and don't be in a division.

Shristi Gurung (12)
Fernhill School, Farnborough

Self-Confidence

This is a message to you, be proud of yourself,
People in your life will forever come and go,
At the end of the day, at least you have yourself,
You are more than enough, you need to realise it,
I know it might be hard to believe it sometimes,
But you just need to have self-confidence always,
Do not let anyone talk down to you or be rude,
Try to gain your confidence, stand up for yourself,
Do not doubt yourself, you have everything right with you,
Don't try to change yourself for anyone, you're enough,
Being the real you is the best you,
You are perfect and amazing,
Stand up for yourself, build up your confidence!

Jessica Shrestha (12)
Fernhill School, Farnborough

Who I Am

I am me,
I keep being judged out in public
without getting to know me,
I hate it.
I am Leah, I am 12
I love music, anime, dancing, having fun
and I like to play video games.
I feel judged because people look at me and
it makes me insecure about myself and
makes me want to change to have people like me.
I have come to realise that I don't need to change cos
I love myself
the only thing that needs to change is
people's perspective of me and
to try to get to know me for me.
Be happy that I am me
but I keep seeing people judging others
just for the way they look.
But just keep being you.

Leah Wheaton (12)
Fernhill School, Farnborough

I Have A Dream

I have a dream,
I have an image.
A hope for a better life,
A hope for the future.

I have a dream,
One where we make a change.
Because we can,
Because we want to.

I have a dream,
One where we live in peace,
In peace with one another,
In peace with Mother Nature.

I have a dream,
Where we all care,
About each other,
About one another.

I have a dream,
One where we are all free.
One where we all have hope,
One where we are what we want to be.

I have a dream,
I have an image.

A hope for a better life,
A hope for the future.

Mariana Pires (12)
Fernhill School, Farnborough

Save The Trees

T reasure you seek within the trees
R abbits hopping inside the leaves,
E verything that I have been
E verything that I have seen

C hange is my middle name
H eart of the tree is my claim
A re the trees dying? "Save the animals," they said
N ever will we ever go through war (animals vs humans)
G et rid of climate change
E verything might just change

W here animals might find light at the end of the tunnel
A nything can come true if you put yourself through the struggle
Y ou can help find the heart within the planet.

Gracie Langford (12)
Fernhill School, Farnborough

Dear Future Me

When the dark descends, get up and resend the message
You read before you were dead.

Dear future me
You gave me hope when I was about to explode
Do not change who you are.
Whatever your gender, everyone stands out.
When I am older, I wish my mum will be proud
No matter the weather, keep doing what you love.
And at last, I see the light.

Dear future me
I will always love the people who helped me get
Through all the tough times.

Dear future me
Find who you are,
Find who you want to be.
If you're not supported, I
Will always support you.

Elizabeth Evans-Holmes (12)
Fernhill School, Farnborough

My Story

Every day I wake up and think I'm not good enough
let people take control and boss me around but I've had enough.

It's time to step up and show who's boss.
Nothing can stop me now, it's time to Floss.

I'm fed up of girls not having equal rights and
people killing themselves.
All the bees and other animals getting shelved.

My parents arguing and getting divorced and no one thinks I'm tough.
My siblings fighting all the time and me getting rough!

But it's time to tell the world that this is me and I am good enough,
No matter what.

Sophie Morris (13)
Fernhill School, Farnborough

To The Person I Knew So Well

To the person I knew so well,
To the one who never fell,
To the girl who played all day,
To the one whose friends would never betray,
All that will go away,
Never to see the light of day,
Once you reach the new school,
You will think yourself a fool
For trusting the ones who made you smile
When all their love wasn't worthwhile,
But this won't last for very long,
For new friends will come along
And when you feel like you're alone,
You'll have new friends to call your own,
So don't give up, you're on your way,
So get some rest and await the day.

Lily Cannon (13)
Fernhill School, Farnborough

Shadows

Dark and lustrous, gleaming under the moon,
Mischievous and mysterious, always walking beside me,
Unknown and silent, staring with gloom.

Always next to me both day and night,
Always keeping me hostage whenever I wander,
Always shady but never glowing bright.

At the strike of dawn, it seems so tall
Endlessly chasing it until I catch up,
But by midday, it becomes somewhat small.

Replicating my movements as I walk along,
Trying to talk to it but never getting a reply back,
Whenever I'm alone, it sings a peaceful yet eerie song.

Harshil Kumar (12)
Fernhill School, Farnborough

Involve You

Why does my diet involve you?
Why do you always make fun of what I eat?
"Oh look, she's eating a burger again."
And your sheep all laugh and tease along with you.

Then when I start skipping meals for what you say,
You comment again, "Eat something, you freak."

I don't understand, you call me fat
And then now you change your mind and call me skinny.
Why can't you choose? I was doing this because of you,
But you make no sense and I don't understand,

Why does my diet involve you?

Izzie Roake (12)
Fernhill School, Farnborough

Change

Does climate change worry you?
If it does, change it
If it doesn't, worry about it
Because the world needs to change
Just think, the animals, the ocean, the land
Every time you litter, chop down trees
You are biting the hand that feeds you
The world doesn't owe you anything
You owe the world everything
If you see someone dropping rubbish
Pick it up and put it in the bin
What you do may be small
But every time you do something small
It becomes something big, something huge
Do it, save the world!

Oliver Lomax (12)
Fernhill School, Farnborough

I Am Shy

I am shy,
I'm not sure why,
But I love being me,
There is no one I would rather be.

From name-calling
To me bawling
Feeling as trapped as can be,
But I love being me.

Feeling as small as a mouse
In my own house,
Feeling as lost as can be,
But I love being me.

From them running away
To me hiding all day,
Feeling as scared as can be,
But I love being me.

I am shy,
I'm not sure why,
But I love being me,
There is no one I would rather be.

Rhianna Fitch (14)
Fernhill School, Farnborough

Dear Future Me, Never Give Up

Dear future me, one thing to ask you,
Be a successful person, even if you want to give up
Get a good job like your parents had.
Dear future me, another thing I ask you,
Buy a nice house and buy a beautiful dog
If he/she is good, give them a nice pat.
Dear future me, another thing to ask you,
Never give up, no matter what cost.
Follow your dreams and make sure you know what to wear.
Dear future me, last thing to ask you,
Never be alone, always have company
When you become successful,
You might find a pair.

Kayden Forder (11)
Fernhill School, Farnborough

YNWA - LFC

You'll never walk alone.
But you'll walk with fear,
As you enter your last game as if saying goodbye,
At the end of this game, it will go bye-bye.
You enter as if a normal game,
But, in fact, it is not.
Wait, it is definitely not normal.
You're in front of the goal,
You think you'll miss,
But wait, you've shot.
It's in! What a goal!
Forty yards!
"You'll never walk alone,"
Finish the fans,
But you'll definitely walk with fear.

Dylan Harris (11)
Fernhill School, Farnborough

My Reflection

I look in the mirror and what do I see?
Sadness, depression, anxiety
I go outside and what do they see?
Happiness, joyfulness and glee
I am who I am and I see what I see
but what is a vision that can't be seen?
I know I am blinded
and can't find the light
but where is my voice?
I can't find my sight
I've been silenced by the world around me
always in a crowd but never seen
isolated with nobody but myself
but the discrimination can't be helped
now I see.

Lexy Musa (12)
Fernhill School, Farnborough

Bunny

Fur as white and fluffy as clouds,
Life with no meaning until he met them,
A boy sweet but oh so shy in the crowds,
Life couldn't get better for the bunny and boy, but then...

Oh, how tragic life can be,
The boy bedridden, sad,
Does God have no sympathy?
Someone gives us some power, even if just a tad.

The bunny oh so lonely, no one to care for it,
If only life wasn't so cruel,
Poor bunny with no love, not even a little bit,
I guess in this world we are just tools.

Sambou-Lamin Jallow (12)
Fernhill School, Farnborough

The Clock

Tick, tock, tick, tock
the clock won't stop
time is always going only forwards
never back
tick, tock, tick, tock
the time, the rhyme, they need to fit in
tick, tick, tock, tock
the change in time
a tick to a tock
and yet it's like years on a clock
round, round, round
tick, tick, tick, tock
if you don't fit in you get rearranged
one part wrong and the rhythm will stop
and yet that stop may be the change we need.

Adam Collins (13)
Fernhill School, Farnborough

Four Baby Guinea Pigs

Four baby guinea pigs all running round,
squeaking and eating, waiting to be put on the grass.
Just wanting to run around and play.

Four baby guinea pigs snuggling their mum and aunties
excited for their salad in the morning,
to munch on carrots, curly kale, apples and more.

When you get picked up, you snuggle into my hands,
as you're getting bigger, now you can't really fit into my hands.
When I see you in the morning, I can see a great future ahead of you.

Millie James (12)
Fernhill School, Farnborough

Dear Future Self

Dear future self,
Remember that you don't have to hide
Always believe in yourself and stand up for what's right

Dear future self,
Remember that you can ask for help
And help others if they need it

Dear future self,
Remember to not let anyone bring you down
Don't let people make fun of you because of who you are

Dear future self,
Most importantly, remember to be true to yourself
Follow your dreams and keep on dreaming!

Vanessa Kaliszewska (12)
Fernhill School, Farnborough

The Spider And Its Web

Spiders!
They can be disgusting
They can be terrifying
Some can be friendly
Some can be deadly
But they make fantastic art
Most spiders make amazing webs
Most webs look like they come out of a canvas
But people kill them
Most people think spiders are deadly creatures
They squish them like a pancake
Spiders only bite if they're scared or annoyed
Most bites are poisonous but
Most don't bite at all
Spiders are wonderful creatures.

Leyland Forder (13)
Fernhill School, Farnborough

Football

One day I wish I am a pro,
Not because I'm scared of being low,
But because I will know
I'm the best,
I will never rest
And I will love success.

One day, I wish I will have fans,
And maybe my face on Coca-Cola cans,
The crowd screaming
And the light beaming,
On me.

I would have signature boots
And expensive suits,
I would be training,
Even if it was raining,
In my garden,
Just like Erling Haaland.

Kye Nielsen (12)
Fernhill School, Farnborough

Dear Future You

Dear future you,
no matter what you are going through,
you will always see it through.
You've come so far,
don't let yourself fall apart.
No matter what you say,
you will always have a way.
Whether you have dreams or not,
never fall down and let your dreams get shot!
Climb your way back up,
and remember that you have luck.
For your fate
I know you will do great.
You will overcome it all,
after all,
I did too.

Angel Wood (12)
Fernhill School, Farnborough

Magic Wand

If I had a magic wand, what would I do,
Would I hide it or share it with you,
Maybe cast a spell,
What would you do?

I waved the wand and made a wish,
Listen carefully and you may hear a swish,
I wish for people to smile,
Although it may take them a while.

One more wish won't hurt a thing,
Remember to enjoy life even though it may sting,
All my wishes are now complete,
Make sure you smile, even if it's down deep.

Rachel Gurung (12)
Fernhill School, Farnborough

Wishes

Now I have three wishes, you'd think this is easy,
a house, a car and a stack of money,
I know this isn't me

now I have three wishes, I wish to heal all,
not just helping myself, being thoughtful,

now I have two wishes, I wish for all to be kind,
and share with the poor,
I could have a car,
but a smile is better if you're thoughtful,

now I have a wish,
I wish for joy to everyone,
now be thoughtful.

Caleb Findlay
Fernhill School, Farnborough

Friends

I once had a friend so good
we met at the top of a car hood.
We talked and talked till noon
then at night we would stare at the moon
but one day I took a step too far
after that, we fell apart
I was really upset
I stared at him when he walked past
I didn't know how long I could last
I thought, *I need to say sorry*, so I did
I went to say hello, but then he just hid
so I just left it alone
and just played at home.

David Gibson (12)
Fernhill School, Farnborough

To My Past Self

To my past self...
Don't listen to the negativity
Don't listen to the people who talk behind your back

Leave the people who don't clap for you when you win
Leave the people who don't listen to you when you speak

Be happy about your image
Don't let people say that you're damaged

Believe in yourself when things go hard
Believe in yourself that you can do it

Just remember you can do it!

Demi Atherton (12)
Fernhill School, Farnborough

Inspiration (Don't Be Afraid)

Don't be afraid to come out and play,
Don't be afraid to say your name,
Give a voice to the ones who don't,
Go out and play to make them strong,
Love the skin you're in!
Love the body you have!

Black or white, you do have rights,
Help and pray to the ones who have been called names,
Let it be free to the ones who need to eat,
Love them whoever they are,
Always do the right thing and
Let them be free.

Max Howells (11)
Fernhill School, Farnborough

Plants

You are a plant pure and true
Although wind won't cause a fright
Don't let storm clouds make you blue
You can always see the light

An acer might be what you are
Losing leaves in the bitter cold
You may think you won't go far
But filled with love you stay bold

Your friend is not just like you
There are many different plants too
Your friend may be tall and high
But you don't need height to fly.

Isis Feldschreiber (12)
Fernhill School, Farnborough

Future Me

Dear future me,
smile even when things are beating you down.

Dear future me,
make your dreams happen
even if you think it's impossible.

Dear future me,
remember who you are
and who loves you for who you are.

Dear future me,
don't let people pull you down
no matter what they do.

Dear future me,
I ask for one last thing,
be safe in that big scary world
ahead of you...

Skye Scoular (12)
Fernhill School, Farnborough

What They Say

They say I'm too big,
they say I'm too small
they say I'm too short,
they say I'm too tall
my spots are everywhere
my scars are showing
they say
but why would I care?
People are people, made to be themselves
why should we care what they say?
Whether you're
big, small
or short, tall
whether you have
acne or scars
you should only care about *you*,
not what they say.

Brooke-Siobhan Boyd (13)
Fernhill School, Farnborough

My Three Wishes For The World

If I had three wishes
I would cure cancer,
So people could enjoy life longer,
And stay with their family until the end.

For my second wish,
I would help the homeless,
I am willing to give a wish for the homeless
So they can have warmth and a home.

For my last wish,
I would help the environment,
So animals could live in their homes still,
And get rid of the plastic that is poisoning the world.

Brooklyn Creed (12)
Fernhill School, Farnborough

Falling In Love

Falling in love is so easy to do,
I fell for you out of the blue.

Hearing your voice and seeing your smile,
You stole my heart and I just went wild.

Feeling your touch and a sweet kiss,
I couldn't help but think that you were my bliss.

Knowing your heart and soul,
This love felt purer than gold.

People may try and rip us apart,
But that will never happen because you have my heart.

Lucy Smith (13)
Fernhill School, Farnborough

My Phone

My phone is my world,
my mum tops up my credit.
I don't know where I'd be without my phone,
a bit like my dog without its bone.

I'm not allowed it in school
which is a stupid rule.
My phone makes me safe, like when it's dark
and I can hear loud barks.

One day my phone will make me millions
whilst the teachers will still be earning pennies
I'm here to be making billions.

Tallulah Carter (13)
Fernhill School, Farnborough

Online Platform

Social media will knock you down
But will never hurt you.

Social media is a bunch of people who are bored
Grown men/women, even children, are mean
Don't let them get in your way.

One day, someone will do it to them
They are a waste of time
You're fine
You are blazing
Because you're amazing.

Just stop worrying about what others think
Just do what you want.

Siyanna Booth
Fernhill School, Farnborough

Dear Past Me

Even if you feel alone,
Don't try to change yourself and roam,
Empower over your shyness and make a friend.

Even if it's getting hard,
Don't try to end the card,
Empower the time we all have.

Even if you don't succeed,
Don't give up on everything you need,
Empower over your fear of being worse.

Dear past me,
Try to be
As positive as you can be.

Daria Gheorghe (12)
Fernhill School, Farnborough

The Secret Blue Curse

If it's black,
If it's blue,
Taller than walls
Maybe it's small

Who knows what it is? I just know that it's cursed,
I wish to tell you but I would simply just burst,
See, that's my issue,
So sick, need a tissue,
I know a secret,
But my curse is to keep it,
There's a crack in my curse, that I can tell you,
The thing has a curse too and its colour is blue.

Sarah Grainger (12)
Fernhill School, Farnborough

Empowered

People don't act serious until they lose something
You have visions but you're still curious
How could you make this world better?
Maybe you have a fear of change, but this is your future,
We can't continue to tear the world,
This world is beautiful, we should spend time to keep it.
Destruction and worry, what will you do in the end?
We must fend for the world before it's too late.

Hayley Atkins-Ramsey (12)
Fernhill School, Farnborough

Future

In my future I will get a job
Don't know what that is yet, but I
Will always think, *never give up.*

I never will give up, I wish to have a good future
I will get a good job.
My past self used to just not care and time flew by.
Still not sure what I will do.

I will dive above the clouds to get a good job
When I'm older, don't care if I fall
Down again.

Anthony Williams (13)
Fernhill School, Farnborough

Empower The World!

Being powerful isn't about being strong,
but about having the ability to rise from the darkness
and show the world that there will always be light
even in the darkest of times.
Being powerful isn't about being the best
but about being the one to lift people up and
show them their potential,
show them that they can be anything they want
and that they should shoot for the stars!

Edward Hinder-Humphrey (13)
Fernhill School, Farnborough

In Football

In football, you need to get shots off
and move the ball quick.
If you don't do good, then you won't get picked.
To play football, you need to have stamina and be slick.
Bend it like Beckham in this 11 v 11
and you know what I reckon?
You can get a good assist.
Shots need to have accuracy and power, and placement
and precision.
Going to a football game is like an expedition.

Jack Packer (12)
Fernhill School, Farnborough

This Is Me

Though I may seem as if I like to yell
really, I'd rather be tucked up in a shell.

Though sometimes I hate all of this,
sometimes sadness takes a swing and receives a miss.

Though sometimes I may seem pretty dim
sometimes my mind hits its swing.

Though most of the time my work isn't that neat,
it's because I'd rather be at home asleep.

Jacob Harrison (11)
Fernhill School, Farnborough

If You Could Have Anything

If you could have anything, what would it be?
Would it be binoculars that help you see
Or doctor equipment to help your knee
Or some seed to help you grow a tree
Maybe a Nerf gun that you can use to play
Or a massive sculpture that's made out of clay
Or a bed where you can rest for the day?
Whether it is clay or a buffet
Whatever it is, it's for you.

Reilly-Jay Sim (12)
Fernhill School, Farnborough

Dear Past Me...

Dear past me...
It's going to be tough,
Trust me, you'll try your best,
A virus called Corona will go around the world,
You'll have to homeschool and it will not be fun.

Dear past me...
You'll be sad but that's okay,
You'll try and it'll make it the best,
Put your hand up in class,
Please, it'll help quite a lot.

Lilly Archibald (11)
Fernhill School, Farnborough

The Way Out

I was too scared to come out of the dark
but someone showed me the way out of the darkness
so I showed the world
the world put me down
but I remembered the way out
so I showed the future the way out
but my past will never find the way out
so I made sure I knew the way out
I helped the people to find the way out
so can you find the way out?

Daniel Jordan (12)
Fernhill School, Farnborough

Dear Future Me

Dear future me, I ask for one thing,
To always take care of yourself,
Dear future me, I ask for one thing,
Always tell the truth, even if the truth will sting,
Dear future me, I ask for one thing,
Take care of the world around you
Because your actions always come back to you.
Dear future me, I ask for one last thing,
To have a successful life.

Harry Badland (11)
Fernhill School, Farnborough

The Perfect Girl

Her blue eyes like the sea.
She is sweet like sugar.
She is gentle like a newborn kitten.

Her hair as bright as the sun.
When she smiles, she makes my day.
Her laugh makes me giggle.

We both have so much in common
like our favourite sport, favourite food and favourite colour.
In this world, there is no love for you like mine.

Kristiyan Traychevski (13)
Fernhill School, Farnborough

Passion

P enalty kick to win, will he sky it or not?
A ccuracy is key, don't know where to shoot.
S trike it with power wherever it goes.
S hot in the top bins
I couldn't believe it! A wonderful penalty
O n the final of the Champions League, to win.
N ever in my life have I ever felt like this.

Jesse Galati (12)
Fernhill School, Farnborough

Rights

Hey you, yes you.
Have you ever been bullied for your size?
Maybe by older girls or guys?
It's not cool or fair.
Well, don't run, just stay there.
Stick up for yourself.
Don't run or hide on a shelf.
Don't give them attention or affection.
Tell someone, get it out.
If they can't hear you then shout.

Oliver Craven (12)
Fernhill School, Farnborough

This Is Me

Dear future me,
I am going to be confident,
not hiding my tears in.

Dear future me,
I am going to speak out, not being afraid.

Dear future me,
I am only asking for one thing,
for everyone to live in peace.

Dear future me,
I want everyone to be treated with respect.

Dear future me.

Maisy-Mai Johnson (11)
Fernhill School, Farnborough

In It Together

Speak out and don't be weak
you will succeed and *they* will feel greed.

Don't you see?
You will be free
for money doesn't buy personality
your right is to fight.

When your fears turn into tears,
make it clear so we can hear
know that you are worth it
and we will help you show it.

Diba Ghafoori (13)
Fernhill School, Farnborough

The Goal

You wake up with fear
not knowing how it goes
you might wonder if you will score any goals
you talk with your teammates
and say, "Play like Bill Gates."
You run towards goal and friends
You say, "I shoot like *Cristianooo...*"
The ball goes top bins
And friends say, "Wow!"

Alfie Taylor Coughlan (11)
Fernhill School, Farnborough

If You Had A Magic Wand, What Would You Do?

If I could cast
a spell of courage
I would make
people change the past

If I could cast
a spell of kindness
I would make people
be nicer than before

If I could cast
a spell of bravery
I would make people
get over a fear of caves

If I could
cast a spell of courage.

Mia Ashwood (12)
Fernhill School, Farnborough

My Three Wishes

If I could wish for one thing every day,
I'd wish for more wishes so they would never go away.

If I could wish for ten things in a year,
I'd wish for good fortune when bad times are near.

If I could wish for one thing with my last wish,
I'd wish to be the winner of the one-hundred-pound gift.

Jack White (12)
Fernhill School, Farnborough

The Real Me

On the outside, this is me
The shy, only-talks-when-he-needs-to me
The not-smart-kid-with-a-blank-face me
The one kid who no one knows or cares about

But on the inside, this is the real me:
The fun, energetic, can't-be-bothered me
The kid who just wants to be a normal person
This is the real me.

Billy Ribton (13)
Fernhill School, Farnborough

My Three Wishes For The World

If I had three wishes,
my first one would be
to cure cancer.

If I had two wishes,
my second one would be
to stop people from committing suicide,
my cousin killed himself when he was fifteen.

If I had one wish,
it would be to help
people who are struggling
in life.

Skye Standing (12)
Fernhill School, Farnborough

To My Past Self

To my past self,
Be proud of yourself
Respect yourself
Just be yourself

To my past self,
Don't care what people think
Only care about what you think
Just be yourself

To my past self,
All you have to do
Is what you want to do
Just... be... your... self.

Holly Miller (12)
Fernhill School, Farnborough

Dear Past Me...

Dear past me,
make sure to smile
because you won't be wanting to
after a while.

A nasty virus
will cover the Earth
and bring it down
to its worst.

If you don't
feel alright,
try to feel okay
because tomorrow,
it will be bright.

Syona Thapa (11)
Fernhill School, Farnborough

Advice For Past Me

Dear past me
I have three requests.

Don't give up
no matter how hard it is
continue as long as it takes.

Take your time
never rush things
because then you will never succeed.

Dream big
you now have the skills
so go forth, little one.

Zack Collins (11)
Fernhill School, Farnborough

Football

F ati plays in the best club
O zil's creativity with the ball
O degaard's free kick, Burnley
T anganga and Zana defence
B alotelli... Agüero, oh my
A ügero, 3-2
L ionel Messi controls
L uis Suárez!

Brandon Munyanyiwa (13)
Fernhill School, Farnborough

I Feel Alive When

I feel alive when the wind is warm and the sky is blue,
I feel alive at the start of something new,
I feel alive when I'm on a roller coaster about to drop down,
When there are butterflies in my stomach not making a sound,
I feel the thrill and excitement,
The rush of it all.

Evie Thompson (11)
Fernhill School, Farnborough

World Wishes

A wish for the world I have
Is for everyone to start anew

A wish for the world I have
Is for everyone to see you

A wish for the world I have
Is for confidence to brew

These three wishes are my commandments.
Obey them and
You will see.

Rocco Cree (13)
Fernhill School, Farnborough

Only For A Day

If you had a wand, what would you do?
Would you give animals back their homes or collect their magic bones?
What about trees being able to grow?
Would you cast a spell of respect and kindness?
Allowing everyone of any race or gender to play?
But only for a day.

Erin Slater (11)
Fernhill School, Farnborough

Angel

Anxious of the way she looks and always worries.
Nervous of always feeling left out from the other angels.
Great service, one of the best-working angels ever to live
Lightens up your world every day
She is such a good angel to be working on the gates of Heaven.

Ellie McAughey (12)
Fernhill School, Farnborough

Favourite Things About Myself

What are my favourite things about myself and also my body?
So, favourite thing about me,
my height because I want to be tall like a model.
My least favourite things are my nose and my eyes
and that's all my favourite things about myself.

Nada Asabam (12)
Fernhill School, Farnborough

My Past And Future

Roses are red
Violets are blue
I hope future me
Becomes something new.

Roses are red
Violets are blue
Primary school was so cool.

Roses are red
Violets are blue
My future dream
Is soon to be true.

Nyla Gorvett (11)
Fernhill School, Farnborough

My Three Wishes For The World

My three wishes,
I wish for equality
so we can all have normality.

I wish for world peace,
so we can all have a piece
of harmony.

I wish for success,
so we can all live a happy life.

Kai Hughes (11)
Fernhill School, Farnborough

My Three Wishes

My three wishes for the world are don't give up when things get tough.
My three wishes for the world are try your best.
My three wishes for the world are don't let people bring you down.

Lily Smith (11)
Fernhill School, Farnborough

World Hunger

My first wish,
end world hunger,
children in pain never getting younger.
My second wish,
cure all disease,
make people healthy,
please, please, please.

Charlotte Rimell (13)
Fernhill School, Farnborough

The Obsidian Wingless Bird

History recalls the 200 million contaminated people carried to God by the heavenly angels,
History recalls when the shackles of Hell latched into our minds,
History recalls the caliginous tendrils of disease as they washed across the land, an indomitable tsunami,
History recalls when the human civilisation was in the clutches of death himself,
History recalls the extremely fatal war that murdered the sinless souls,

History recalls when this serial killer left, leaving a permanent trauma,
History recalls the blackened tissues spreading like the illuminated shadow throughout England,
History recalls bodies deteriorating, leaving the one depleted land an obsolete graveyard,
History recalls the apocalypse of rats and flies contaminating the victims,
History recalls the bird of black in a wingless coat, sweeping thousands to the grave for eternity,
History recalls everyone dispensing with their souls as they inched toward God,

History recalls, it repeats itself, as the pandemic (Coronavirus) dawns upon us,
History recalls the Black Death.

Ashmeet Kaur (13)
Seva School, Coventry

Missing You

I keep recalling the day you left,
Drowning in tears, this would be a real test,
Remembering you, so interested in your Bollywood shows and movies too
I'm still missing you.

Visiting you almost every weekend,
When we stopped going to your house,
It was a real challenge.
Your warm, comforting hug made me feel safe,
Not feeling that anymore makes me feel blue,
I'm still missing you.

Don't think I forgot about you,
Seeing you in Leicester,
In your house I always see something new!
Whenever I saw you, you had a warm bright smile too,
I'm still missing you.

I couldn't imagine life without you,
You waiting at my grandma's house
For a family gathering or event.
When we do that now, it is not the same,
It makes everyone blue,
I'm still missing you.

Laila Heer (12)
Seva School, Coventry

Sikh History Through The Ages

Jaggi Singh Johal: may your soul live on
he's been tortured; morphed from a man
out of his mind to a man of religion.

Saint Jarnail Singh Ji Khalsa Bhinderawale was
a man of religion,
he was a man who witnessed complete division.
1984 massacre: why did they close their doors
after?

West Midland 3 had their houses broken
into:
their families were scarred, going straight to
the remnants of history.

In 1978, our brothers were killed
no reason for it; we had been drilled.
Khalistan, we hope to live as long
why are we portrayed as completely wrong?

Why is there no equality?
We've always been a fraternity.
Blue Star didn't get far.
We secured our Darbar.

Eashar Singh (13)
Seva School, Coventry

A New Dawn After The Dark

Darkness,
It is present,
It's what the humans dread

Darkness,
It can hold the unknown,
And your deepest fears

Darkness,
Not only does it take over the sky,
It can also reside in your mind

Darkness,
Though not always noticed,
It can just stick by

But after the darkness,
Will come the light

Just like the day,
Comes after the night

A new day will come,
A new day will rise

And a new hope for humanity,
Will come to life

We will fight the darkness,
As the pandemic sways

Even though we lose our family and friends,
We will be determined to stay

So tell the darkness,
A big goodbye

As we fight to live,
And not to die.

Annanya Gupta (12)
Seva School, Coventry

Women's Rights

Why did women have to stay home?
Why could women not work?
Why are women told no?
Why do women get hurt?

Who said women aren't capable?
Who said women are inferior?
Who said women can't do it?
Who said women aren't worth it?

Why do women have to suffer?
Why do women get the pain?
Why do women have to fight?
Why do women have to hide?

Who said women aren't strong?
Who said women aren't brave?
Who said women should stay home?
Who said women couldn't play sports?

Women are capable!
Women are strong!
Women are equal!
Women are worth it!

Ria Virat (13)
Seva School, Coventry

Dear Current Generation...

Dear current generation,
Times right now have been tough,
We have been in turmoil, struggling quite a lot,
But don't let someone bring you down,
Follow your dreams and be yourself.

Dear current generation,
We were like warriors fighting a battle,
We overcame the challenge,
We overcame our fear,
We put on a brave face,
Refusing to let the virus win.

Dear future generation,
Understand the pain that we faced,
So learn from this and take our advice,
Like an ambitious warrior who never gives up,
So you and me must learn from this war and stay strong.

Savneet Singh (13)
Seva School, Coventry

Jaswant Singh Khalara

Reminiscing about the
victories our Sikh forefathers fought
for.
Fighting against shackles, a
principle we fought
for.
Death was near and
God's sanctuary was guaranteed.
Fighting like lions rising to
sovereignty.
Breaking bonds of
fear and death.
Sticking to Maryada.
Called sons of turmoil
we were belittled and killed, that's
what they saw:
avenging the deaths, that's
what they swore.

Through fighting legal
cases, they
expelled the dark
empowered a light.
One that shone far...

Jaswant
Singh
Khalara.

Kataar Singh Khalsa (12)
Seva School, Coventry

What Is Going On In The World?

What is going on in the world that makes people happy or angry?
What should people know about?

Love it or hate it,
how does education empower you?

Give a voice to those who don't have one
Who inspires you, what do you aspire to be or do?

Does climate change worry you?
What about endangered species facing extinction?
Are you environment-friendly?
Can you persuade others to be with your words?

What's it like to be you?
What makes you feel empowered, strong and confident?
What's it like to be the one who inspires people?

Zakariye Bile (11)
Seva School, Coventry

She

Hands tied,
tied tight.
She cried,
he lied.

He controlled her life,
making her his wife.
She could not control her life,
which made her his wife.

She waited for her hero,
or she could be her own hero.
Then she heard her calling,
her thoughts came pouring.

She rose like Emily Pankhurst,
a pioneer, one of the first.
Finally, she was all alone,
no more listening to her husband's moans.

Us women are strong,
us women are brave.
No need to put us down,
as we will make our way around.

Raman Kaur Bains (13)
Seva School, Coventry

At Least I Try

"Do better," they say, hiding all the jealousy.
Not trusting anyone, I got no chemistry.
I try again and again, got no energy,
Living a life full of negativity,
Positivity? Never heard of that.
But now I know I'm getting better at the fact
That I don't give up.
Showing people how to love.
If they don't learn, it ain't my fault,
They can go hide in a vault,
I'm out there, practising,
Showing off all the things I learnt from literacy,
At least I try.
I don't lie.
The one who reaches the sky.

Khushmeet Brar (13)
Seva School, Coventry

Anokh Singh Babbar

Anokh Singh Babbar,
He was torn apart,
Tortured for days,
And lived for his part.

Anokh Singh Babbar,
They lived for Shaheedi,
Holding an AK-Santali,
They fought till the end
And didn't mind Diwali.

Anokh Singh Babbar
Avenged the Singhs,
He fought hard
And never gave in.

Anokh Singh Babbar
Nitnem every day,
Amritvela, Naam Japna,
"Vand ke chakna," he used to say.

Anokh Singh Babbar,
They have been shaheed,
But their valour still remains
In our veins.

Jasjeevan Bhachu (12)
Seva School, Coventry

Positive Emotions

Everyone has his or her happy moments,
My best happy moment was my big birthday party.
It was one of the best.
I loved it so much.

I am so joyful of the things God has done for me
He helped me succeed in my whole life.

Victorious, I have been victorious in my graduations
In school and many promotions too.

I am also so delighted because of what my God
Has done for me, the gift of life, and also helped
Me succeed in my last examination in primary
With a Super 1 grade!
I am so thankful for him in all.

Theresa Nakidde (14)
Seva School, Coventry

We Can Change The Planet Together!

- **E** veryone needs to participate to keep Earth clean. Every day we look around and see less blue and green.
- **A** lways recycle and pick up litter, anyone can prevent climate change, even by spreading awareness on Twitter.
- **R** eversing climate change isn't 'doable' - reducing climate change by using fuels that are renewable.
- **T** oday we will start changing our lifestyle. Tomorrow we will carry on so not too many problems start to pile.
- **H** igh temperatures are killing our planet. However, we can still change our daily habits.

Ajooni Kaur Bahra (13)
Seva School, Coventry

The 2020 Disaster

2020 carried a few surprises,
the lockdown, COVID-19, online school,
"Vaccine,"
"Vaccine,"
did they do anything?

Schools shutting down were a big mess,
"You're behind on work," well, no one explained the task,
this generation has been through a flop.

The Earth has been destroyed,
global warming, littering and pollution,
we are slowly killing the Earth and ourselves,
we must learn how to take care of things well,
or we might just wipe out our planet...

Heavenpreet Kaur (11)
Seva School, Coventry

Freedom

Sant Jarnail Singh Bhindranwale Ji gave the Sikhs freedom.
We're the ones who had the light to bring back our earldom.
Operation Blue Star happened in 1984.
That was the time where we had to cope with bad laws.
Indira Gandhi was the PM at the time,
We were blamed for all the crimes.
We had the right to speak up for ourselves,
But the PM just took it all for herself.

Darkness started to invade the Punjab.
We Sikhs had been given an alarm,
To bring equality to the world
And follow the Lord.

Rajinder Gill (12)
Seva School, Coventry

Dear Future Me

Dear future me,
Follow your dreams whatever happens.
Love yourself, you are perfect
Don't be sad, look for the positive

Dear future me,
If you ever get bullied, talk, you will get better
If you ever get body-shamed, remember you are perfect the way you are
If you ever get sad, know you can find happiness anywhere

Dear future me,
Know you are perfect
Chase your dreams, you'll catch them
Look at the positive side, you'll be happy
Respect yourself, you are expensive.

Sophie Teplicka (11)
Seva School, Coventry

The Future Me!

Dear future me,
One thing I ask of you,
No matter how hard things get,
You never give up on anything!
Follow your dreams, no matter how bad things seem
And try to see them through

Dear future me,
I ask of you one thing,
If you have any problems,
Just talk to a trusted person,
Don't be afraid to admit how you feel.

Dear future me,
One thing I ask of you,
Remember to stay happy,
And smile every day!

Reetdeep (11)
Seva School, Coventry

More Love, No Hate

More love, no hate
More equality, no hate
More kindness, no hate
More gender equality, no hate.

Let's get rid of the hate in this world all together
Now until eternity, now and forever.

From hate and racism to bullying and gender prejudice.
And let's turn it into love and equality
To kindness and gender equality.

Let's get rid of the hate in this world all together
Now until eternity, now and forever.

Avleen Mann (12)
Seva School, Coventry

Thank You

Today is the day that I praise the people who fought with me along the way,
Thank you, because you taught me your way,
You helped me when I cried and whined,
Thank you, I made you proud,
You watched me grow and now I know how important you are,
We went through a lot and I got what I wanted.
Thank you, I'm grateful for everything you have done,
Because in every woman and man, there are some people called Mom and Dad.

Robert Chiscan (11)
Seva School, Coventry

Gender Equality

We say we have gender equality in today's society,
but do we really?

Yes, women can be a part of the working world,
and yes, women can be leaders out there.
But behind this great disguise
lies the bitter, cold truth.

All around the world,
women are treated like dirt and soil
just because of who they are.
Why should we be ashamed of who we are?

Why should we feel any less?

Ekamjot Kaur (14)
Seva School, Coventry

Fight Against Climate

The fight against climate change is near to a final.
Life on Earth is close to an end,
Global warming might be near,
But climate change is already here,
We'll see our sun and moon.
But what about our trees and plants?
Mother Earth is no longer thriving,
Everyone keeps on chilling.
Nothing but pollution fills our air,
No one seems to care.
We've flooded our air with the deadliest poison.

Eesha Kaur
Seva School, Coventry

The King Of Pop (Michael Jackson)

Songs sold
and worlds told,
only phrases of gold
are allowed
that make you proud.

We gained
the words of him:
"Look at yourself and make
a change,"
he wanted you to say,
turn around and not be
afraid.

The man M J
made us not sad
but happy,
not bad,
not mad,
but now he is
deceased.
We wish him well.
Rest in
peace.

Arjun Dhillon (12)
Seva School, Coventry

Don't Underestimate The Power Of A Mother

You have sent your hope
Your love
Your life
You have picked me up when I was low.
You're always there left and right
And made sure I know everything I know.
You have wiped my tears
You have given me power to survive through life
And picked me up when I fell.
You are the best role model.
I did this to say thank you
And that our endless love never ends
I love you, Ma.

Jaya Kaur (11)
Seva School, Coventry

Free Jaggi

He made a website for what was right,
But didn't know it would cause a fright,
Free Jaggi, free Jaggi now.

His arrest raised an eyebrow,
Life for him is tough right now,
Free Jaggi, free Jaggi now.

Tortured every day,
Left to decay,
Free Jaggi, free Jaggi now.

Put in a place
Where light doesn't have a say,
Free Jaggi, free Jagtar Singh Johal.

Jugraj Singh Bening (12)
Seva School, Coventry

If I Had A Magic Wand

If I had a magic wand,
I would have stopped COVID,
It would cure everyone quicker,
Instead of using the vaccine.

If I had a magic wand,
I would stop global warming,
It would help the people from these disasters,
And they will never panic again.

If I had a magic wand,
I would stop poverty,
They will never suffer,
And they will be happy again.

Austin Jaison (11)
Seva School, Coventry

The Extinct Animal

The animal kingdom is very vast,
but this one is the very last.
These safe animals remaining, one animal in the world is the Tasmanian Devil
but now there are none.
When they remained,
there were lots of hunters that came.
They couldn't escape very fast,
this was in the past.
Seeing the sadness,
the sun glared,
the moon murmured,
the Earth agreed.

Manreet Baidwan (12)
Seva School, Coventry

The Person Who Gave Me Life

To the person who gave me life,
you have done more than make me strive.

To the person who gave me life,
if I lose you, I will sting like a bee in a hive.

To the person who gave me life,
I remember when I used to help you peel the potatoes with a knife.

I may soon have a wife,
but I will never forget you,
the person who gave me life.

Benjamin Doherty (11)
Seva School, Coventry

This Is My Say

This is my chance
To say my say.
This is my day...

I started off happy,
Then they said my life was gappy,
I want people to know the real me
Since this day,
This is my say.

But I kept my chin up high,
Still looking up at the sky,
I'm going to be me,
So I say,
Tomorrow is 'me' day.

Jeevan Kaur (11)
Seva School, Coventry

Inspirational Life

You are the one
Who will never be gone,
You inspired me,
You never let me down,

You kept me safe,
There was no case,
You gave me the strength,
You gave me the help,

You taught me how to learn,
You taught me how to earn,
You taught me how to survive,
Thank you for everything.

Gurmehar Maan (12)
Seva School, Coventry

Have Hope

Achieve the goals in your life,
Fight your fears,
Do not shed any tears,
Solve your problems of any length,
Do not give up, and show your strength,
Inspire people wherever you are,
Life is like an unstoppable car,
Believe in yourself and follow your dreams,
Nothing is as hard as the way it seems.

Gursheen Kaur (11)
Seva School, Coventry

Empowered

- **E** mbrace equality
- **M** otivate other people
- **P** erpetuate happiness
- **O** ptimistic always
- **W** itty
- **E** thical
- **R** ectify bad feelings
- **E** voke joy
- **D** estroy negativity.

Dev Atwal (13)
Seva School, Coventry

The Sea Is All We Need

The sea is
our king
we feed from you
we shouldn't throw trash in you
we should just leave you
we love the crystal, glistening lagoon
we should be tight together
and live a normal life together.

Bailee Humphrey (13)
Seva School, Coventry

My Dream

D reaming means to never say 'no',
R emember equality,
E xcellence in life,
A spire and inspire,
M ean what you say.

Zayed Al-Aamery (11)
Seva School, Coventry

Forbidden Love

This wasn't supposed to happen,
You're my innocent hope but I am a tragic assassin
I admire those with pupils that shine purity, blinding my sinner eyes
I try to amend my mistakes from centuries ago but all I touch dies with my lies
We were opposite but the things I risked just to see your face beam euphoria
Whilst mine leaked dysphoria,
I concealed my presence in the obsidian shadows
Whilst the founded were shot with agonising arrows
My people hated yours
But you were my only ever cure
When our eyes met each other
This unbearable pain engulfed us both, knowing our love would only lead to great suffering
So why did you stand before me
To the point crimson blood was all I could see?
The moments we savoured and craved, knowing we were never going to truly be
We strolled through the enchanted forests, hiding from guards we could see
But we felt completely free
So, my love, why would you sacrifice your soul?
For someone who's anger spirals out of control
I still remember to this day

When that serrated blade pierced through your pale skin
that now stains a raging red
Because now you are dead
Monstrous pain clumped inside my throat, slowing,
suffocating me, narrowing my last breaths
This feeling infuriated me with inflamed stress
This burden stays with me to this very day
When I carried you home with my bloody arms but failed to keep you safe
My eyes bleed when thinking about your precious smile and daring acts that kept me awake
What can I say? Opposites attract
But this time, the evil survives and tells the story
Whilst the hero rests in the heaven's glory.

Maninder Bains (12)
The Khalsa Academy Wolverhampton, Ettinghshall

My Greatest Hero Is He

Took electric dreams and made them come true,
Mars atmosphere his car drove through.
He plans our survival all the while,
They attack his business and call him vile.
So if one makes oneself judge the measures of Elon's worth,
Give him his humanity and understand him first.

So while you pose your list of what his failings may be,
Remember his emotions prove he's just like you and me.
My greatest hero is he.
Since he's my hero, my weight is less than zero.
He wants to send us to Mars
In a bunch of electric cars.
For his, mine and mankind's dream,
He dreamt of them as a child by the streams.

My greatest hero is he.
He lands his rockets near the sea.
Like Isaac Newton and his tree.
His life isn't actually with glee.
He's married to three!
And sadly lost his firstborn,
Since that, he has sworn
To change the world.
My greatest hero is he.

Before you wish him failure or Twitter him your hate,
Be mindful, his great intentions just might save us from fate.
My greatest hero is he.

Sukhmanpreet Preet Singh (14)
The Khalsa Academy Wolverhampton, Ettinghshall

First Day Of Secondary School

It's scary when you're starting school
And you must be afraid
Don't worry too much about this 'new'
You will get used to it, you'll make friends

You will make new companions and learn much more
You can find even old friends in the school corridor!
Everything is different so you think you're lost
Nothing to worry about, you will get the best.

New teachers, new students, everything's unfamiliar to you.
Seems like a different life, maybe it's true.
Concentrate on your journey, beginnings are light
It will help you achieve your goals, you will turn just right.

Get back on your feet and stand for yourself!
Behave and be respectful, and expect at least the same.
Have a quality start, start this current voyage like a model
Take advantage of your ability, no reason to hide.

Be as courageous as you've always been and are
Confidence is the key to this new start.
Be yourself, I know you absolutely can.
Rise and shine, you have a chance to grow again.

Lorena Mihai (11)
The Khalsa Academy Wolverhampton, Ettinghshall

War Zone

As new men came in, you heard screaming,
While we were in our beds, dreaming,
Men came so badly hurt,
Whilst others were even burnt!
Here I am as a nurse,
When the bullets were about to burst
I miss my home,
Yet here I am, treating bones.

I am a nurse, this is me
When I know others at home will be dancing in jubilee,
The soldiers fighting for our country,
How brave they are bound to be!
Out there, soldiers are dying on the battlefield
When at home this is all concealed.

How sad it must have been
For the families at home to see
Their loved ones dying at the scene
Traumatised they would've been.
Here there is no sun,
For this war is yet still to be won.
Here I am, working in the war
For the soldiers that have been torn.

Aanya Mahey (12)
The Khalsa Academy Wolverhampton, Ettinghshall

Serendipity

Lonely,
Isolated
I was...
Drowned in an ocean of
Darkness, no hope, no light,
No colour
Was there,
It was just dark and sad...
No light could reach,
No hope was felt,
No euphoria ever existed
In that solitary cell.

But
There was someone,
Ambitious, mysterious
And bright,
He was just...
He wasn't in darkness,
Unlike me,
He was the bright star,
Free and eternal to live.

He is the hope,
The bright in the forest,

The reflection of light
In the drawing room.

No mortal creature
Could replace him,
He is the only one
To bring euphoria,
To take dysphoria,
To being helpful to this planet,
Led up to peace,
Just and just for me,
Me
And me...

The feeling of epiphany
That you made me realise,
The serendipity
That you brought in my life
Would be forever,
And we're eternal...

Ritika Kumari (14)
The Khalsa Academy Wolverhampton, Ettinghshall

Cheating Chance

Heads or tails?

I thought for a while,
Considering fully my reply,
I plastered on a smile
As I stared at the sky.

Heads, and I fail
As I always tend to do
Tails, and perhaps this will be the tale
Of one of my rare passing few.

Heads, and reality hurtles back
With its devilish little grin.
Tails, and the world lifts from black,
Coloured from my one major win.

Heads, and they say no,
Another for the rejection list.
Tails, and maybe I can go
In a miraculously fated twist.

Heads, and I take the dive
Into murky waters beneath me,
Tails, and I'm still alive
And quite possibly free.

"Tails," I finally say
And head down it lay,
The coin is then pocketed away,
Knowing I chose another day.

Ravneet Kaur (15)
The Khalsa Academy Wolverhampton, Ettinghshall

Apologise

Showed up not even a minute late
Time goes on on its own
Without a single apology
Joyous laughs and eccedentesiasts
The serendipity I was looking for was false
Until I met her smile, elysian eyes
In the scintilla.
Across the dream, past the woods
I'm going to the place that's getting clearer
Seeing the darkness through the dandelions.
Surrounded by eleutheromania,
I still had to be alone.
There are too many voices talking
But even if the sandy ocean floor split into two
Everyone if someone shaded up their world
I'll never let go his freedom
He's the cause of my euphoria.

Harleen Kaur (14)
The Khalsa Academy Wolverhampton, Ettinghshall

Next Generation

Dear next generation,

Roses are red,
Violets are blue,
This is the world
That belongs to you!

This world is full of surprises,
Bad and good, I'll tell you about it,
This is the poem for the next generation,
Take good care of God's creation,

Recycle plastic and make the world a better place.
Be a good guy instead of judging race.

In your life, there are going to be difficulties.
Run through them all and you'll make your way to royalties.

Never let anyone tell you different!

Vanshvir Singh (11)
The Khalsa Academy Wolverhampton, Ettinghshall

A Drop Of A Tear

A drop
of a tear is
like a pool of rain.
Knock at the door, my heart's
full of pain. Unexpected, but often
welcomed with a frown. They can brighten
your day or ruin your plans. They can come
when you laugh or make you sad, only then do you
get people's attention. A teardrop holds many secrets,
it's a bubble of anticipation. It can cleanse the
Earth and feed the flowers. The teardrop is
never silent. It bangs against your face,
your clothes, into people.
A drop of a tear.

Sharan Kaur (17)
The Khalsa Academy Wolverhampton, Ettinghshall

Possession

Blood dripped down her collarbone,
Pain shook her body.
Each letter was covered in blood,
It looked beautiful on her skin.

The name carved into her skin represented their love.
Their love so strong,
Cannot be broken by binds.
And cannot be forced by chains.

She knew what it meant,
What it meant to be his.
She belonged to him,
Him and him only.

Parminder Kaur (11)
The Khalsa Academy Wolverhampton, Ettinghshall

It's Halloween!

Halloween time is finally here,
So all you scaredy-cats, it's time to fear!
For all the demon spirits and pumpkins alight are now near,
You can run but not hide, my dear!

Here you are, dressed up for the night,
When the moon is full and bright,
You knock and knock, hoping to fright,
Trick or Treat? I call at your door, it's Halloween Night!

Chanpreet Chouhan (11)
The Khalsa Academy Wolverhampton, Ettinghshall

What It's Like To Be You

It's always the best to be you!
You should never change yourself for anyone.
You should always be you!
Don't change your identity, your looks, your personality
for anyone.
You should be you!
You should be the best version of you
not anyone else.
You are only competing for yourself, not anyone else!
Be you, not anyone else!

Simran Kaur (11)
The Khalsa Academy Wolverhampton, Ettinghshall

The Watery Ocean

Waves just being waves,
All the ocean names:
Atlantic, Pacific, Indian and Arctic,
Antarctic too.

Each one with a borderline,
Having a nice swimming time,
In the oceans fish stay,
In the end, they will all be prey.

Dive under the waves,
Into the sea,
Look at the sunny days,
Why don't you come with me?

Ishaan Singh Aujla (11)
The Khalsa Academy Wolverhampton, Ettinghshall

World War I And World War II

World War I and World War II,
When they got out, bullets flew.
Bodies dropped and bullets rained,
Gunfire continued while men were slayed.

World War I was where it started,
Nazis fought and bullets pierced.
Out soldiers fell and the lives perished,
In our hearts we will never forget it.

Jassraj Singh (11)
The Khalsa Academy Wolverhampton, Ettinghshall

Dear Global Warming...

It always struck hotter and hotter
and the Earth can end because of you.

Global warming...
It always gets hotter and hotter
and it will soon burn my back off.

Global warming...
Our future may go dark because of you
destroying the world.

Armaandeep Patara (13)
The Khalsa Academy Wolverhampton, Ettinghshall

Family Are Better Than Friends!

Inspired by Dominic Toretto

Family are better than friends.
Friends could be the fake ones.
Families are the same blood as you.
Friends could take other people's sides instead of yours.
Some friends are loyal, some are unmerciful.
Family are better than friends.

Paramveer Singh (11)
The Khalsa Academy Wolverhampton, Ettinghshall

Dreams

Life without dreams
what should I do?
Life without dreams
what will I do?
Should I go here?
Should I go there?
But my dreams are to be...
everywhere!

Aditya Singh (11)
The Khalsa Academy Wolverhampton, Ettinghshall

Empowered

What does 'empowered' mean?
Supporting and encouraging someone to be stronger and confident.

I wanted to fly to the sky
ride in the wind
but now I want to glide on the ice.

The centre and wings, skating with sticks
they skate really quick
on the ice, no one's a bore
we love to score.

On the ice, I feel free
sometimes I also skate through the trees.
The falls and fails that happened all night,
I never stopped till I gave them a fright.

The love I feel with my team
it all feels like a dream.
Crowds screaming and chanting,
we all flee to the locker rooms, jamming.

It's now after half-time
I'm feeling empowered with strength
we touch the ice to remember his death,
John, our beloved coach.

Summer Button (14)
Treorchy Comprehensive School, Pengelli

Empowered

When do you feel safe?
You may feel safe with friends, family or significant others.
You may feel safe in a place close to your heart -
I feel safe in my room. Isolated.
Because that is how people have made me feel.
"Your hair is dirty."
"Your teeth are yellow."
"Ew, look at her clothes."
I feel safe in my room because I'm away from people.
"She's going to Hell if she's gay."
"I don't want people like her near me."
So I find my safe place.
If you are going through anything like this,
Find where you feel safe too.
My home is filled with love.
My mother, my father, my sister, my dogs,
They make me feel safe.
But I isolate myself.
"Go back to your country."
"Why does she talk like that?"
"She's too loud."
But the love I get from my safe place empowers me.
I'm different.
I'm not the same as you.
And I'm okay with that because I'm my own person.

I'm unique.
You are too.
I reached out from the shadows I was forced into and found people who include me,
People who understand me,
And most importantly, people who accept me.
So reach out,
Find people who make you feel safe, loved and alive.
You can only hide in the shadows so long.
And let me tell you,
Once you're out you will never want to go back in.

Layla Van Zijl (13)
Treorchy Comprehensive School, Pengelli

Perfection

Some want a girl
With blonde hair as blonde as sand,
But I don't, I have brown like mud

Others want a young woman
With sharp blue eyes as blue as the sky,
But I don't, I have grey, as grey as a storm

More want a female
Who is tall, as tall as 5" 9,
But I'm not, I'm only middle size

Lots want a lady
With an athletic figure as strong as a mountain,
But I'm not, I'm skinny and lanky

Few want a damsel
With cupid-bow lips as red as an apple,
But I don't have, mine are pale

Most want a gal
With long, long lashes as lengthy as a thumbnail,
But mine aren't, mine are half the size

Many want a skirt,
With manicured nails as pretty as a rose,
But mine aren't, they're bitten

The majority want a lass
With long curly hair curled like a confetti,
But mine isn't, mine is bushy.

No less want a girlie
With a bit of a tan as dark as coffee,
But I'm not, I'm pale

But only a few want a beauty
To have a kind, creative personality as sweet as chocolate,
And to look and be themselves as bold as neon

And I've got those, as natural as Earth,
For my mother birthed me like this,
And this is what I am, free to be me.

Jamie-Lee Taylor (15)
Treorchy Comprehensive School, Pengelli

I See A Girl

When you look in a mirror what do you see?
I see a girl who wants to be accepted
A girl who is different
A girl who hides behind the face.

I see a girl who, despite her home life,
Tries her hardest to make a better life for herself
A girl who although seems happy is okay
Cries herself to sleep at night.

I see a girl who if given the chance,
To change anything about herself
Would change everything
Just to look and feel perfect.

I see the insecurities
The self-hate
The imperfections
The scars of her school life.

I see a girl who doesn't like her life
Who doesn't want to feel imperfect and wasteful
A girl who plasters a smile on to avoid questions
Who pulls her head underwater just to feel *alive*.

I see a girl who even though covers up so well
Still lets the mask slip now and again

A girl who hears people's opinions
A girl who acts like the comments don't affect her

But if you don't speak out it chips away at you
Until suddenly there's no fight left.

Molly-Jo Carmichael (13)
Treorchy Comprehensive School, Pengelli

Empowered

Dear future me,

don't worry.
All things will happen if they are meant to,
stop comparing the past to the present.
You left it behind for a reason,
so go forward confidently into the future you are developing right now.

Keep smiling...
Those small worries and concerns will be forgotten in a year's time.
Be thankful for those small blessings that grace your life each day.
Even when it seems things are falling apart,
it takes destruction of all the old to build up the new.

One day,
all the invisible strings holding those things in the sky aloft will be served
and the things will all come crashing down to Earth below to shatter into a million pieces
and the world will be covered with moon dust and star remands,
and we will still be here in one way or another,
terrified and terrifying observers of the end of our sky.

Wherever you are right now
let it teach you something,
be kind to yourself on the journey
and in the process of who you are becoming...

Kayleigh Perry (14)
Treorchy Comprehensive School, Pengelli

The Empowerment Of Women

I once read the lines:
'Practically on top of us
is a girl
with long blonde hair,
a tight, fitting dress
and the nicest patents I have ever seen.'
I automatically dislike her
for that outfit
a harsh reminder
of my unadorned looks
that shall evermore linger.

This mentally troubles me
for no one should perceive
they aren't superior enough
for this detestable society with endure.

Why can't we admire
another's beauty, so perceptible
instead of becoming covetous
or desirous of it?
We can't find a flaw
for there are none
to discover in these beguiling women.

Perhaps I shall soon perceive
that we are all together unblemished
perhaps I shall soon discern
that we are all equivalent.

We need to empower each other
for everyone deserves the same
no matter who they might be.

Ella Davies (15)
Treorchy Comprehensive School, Pengelli

As It Is You Are Perfect

A s I gazed into the mirror
S tared down those eyes once more

I realised and recognised something
T hat I had never seen before

I n those big round eyes
S omewhere, tucked away,

Y ou can find a feeling
O f reassurance and array
U nder the exterior skin

A bove the organic insides
R elaxation lives in peace
E ducating the mind to harmonise

P eople and pets give me joy
E very single day
R apidly increasing my mental health
F orever making sure I'm gay
E very day is a new opportunity
C atch it and get immunity
T o help your community.

Cecilia Horvath-Vass (12)
Treorchy Comprehensive School, Pengelli

Empowered

What does empowered mean?
Supporting and encouraging someone to be stronger and confident

You empower me
You help me, like a swaying tree in the wind
You keep me happy, you keep me dry
So thank you, my friend, for all your support

We fought together
We lived together
You kept me sane, you kept me real
So thank you, my friend, for all your support

You kept true to yourself, loved yourself
You never let anyone tear you down
You were the best friend anyone could've hoped for
So thank you, my friend, for all your support.

Without you, I'd be lost, forgotten, irrelevant.
Without you, I'd be disregarded.
So thank you, my friend,
For all your support.

Leo Lanciotti (13)
Treorchy Comprehensive School, Pengelli

Difference

'Tiny', 'small',
Harmless little words,
Yet damage dealt is damage felt
Deep within our heart,

'Creep', 'weirdo', 'freak',
Disabilities shouldn't embarrass,
Yet damage dealt is damage felt
Deep within our heart,

'Alien', 'strange', 'unhuman',
We have a right for our own kind of relationship,
Yet damage dealt is damage felt
Deep within our heart,

From the outside we're all different,
But on the inside we're some part the same,
How we appear can't be hidden forever,
So don't make fun of us for something
We can't change.

Lilien Horvath-Vass (12)
Treorchy Comprehensive School, Pengelli

Equal Rights

Long ago, women were born to cook and clean,
Expected to marry and have a child when still a teen.
No rights, no say, our opinions put aside
In the country we lived in, to a man's law we must abide.
Didn't matter if we were to show intelligence or potential,
Our opinions still deemed to be unessential.
We received the right to vote in 1918,
However, things are still not quite as they seem.
I still won't get paid as much as a man,
But can I fight for my rights? Indeed, I can.
Just remember, the war of rights isn't over yet,
Keep on fighting your battles, and justice we shall get.

Millie Hislop (14)
Treorchy Comprehensive School, Pengelli

New Page

Do you feel empowered? Yes or no?
Because if you don't, then you should open a new door
Turn over a page, a new chapter in life
If everyone's a fork then you be a knife
Take opportunities and risks to feel alive
Set ambitions and goals, then drive
Drive towards ambitions
Drive towards goals
And watch while everyone who doubted you falls
They will all watch you, filled with rage
And all of this because you turned over a new page.

Ieuan Jones (14)
Treorchy Comprehensive School, Pengelli

Empowered - Animal Extinction: Nick The Last Whale

The last of the group,
Majestic and humongous,
He strides elegantly through the deep, endless sea.

He makes his last call,
Hoping for an answer but not expecting one.

The plastic consoles his body,
He reminisces about his lost family
Who he once smiled with.

He takes his last breath,
Now he shall rest.

Speak up,
Do better,
Empower.

Katie Williams (14)
Treorchy Comprehensive School, Pengelli

The Forging

The iron fell to the mould
the dark room flashes
each second that passes
you think of the life you live
an identity forged by others
it's not who you are
with each clash of hammer to blade
the life you've left
a lot forged by others
ideas forged by others
the life that is new
forged by you.
The final strike dies
and standing there is a new you.

Trystan Rogers (13)
Treorchy Comprehensive School, Pengelli

YoungWriters® Est. 1991

YOUNG WRITERS INFORMATION

We hope you have enjoyed reading this book – and that you will continue to in the coming years.

If you're the parent or family member of an enthusiastic poet or story writer, do visit our website **www.youngwriters.co.uk/subscribe** and sign up to receive news, competitions, writing challenges and tips, activities and much, much more! There's lots to keep budding writers motivated!

If you would like to order further copies of this book, or any of our other titles, then please give us a call or order via your online account.

Young Writers
Remus House
Coltsfoot Drive
Peterborough
PE2 9BF
(01733) 890066
info@youngwriters.co.uk

Join in the conversation!
Tips, news, giveaways and much more!

YoungWritersUK   YoungWritersCW   youngwriterscw